Stairways, Fountains, and Streetlights
The Urban Details Series

Stairways, fountains and streetlights are among the many overlooked small things that beautify our cities and give them character. Noticing and appreciating them is the idea behind the Urban Details series. Many have significant histories and are associated with important civic leaders, many are merely the result of some functional requirement, but nearly all are the loving creations of anonymous artisans.

Discover the "Music Box" steps where Laurel and Hardy rolled a grand piano up a long stairway in this Academy Award-winning film. Imagine corseted high-heeled housewives negotiating hundreds of narrow steps heading to the streetcar carrying shopping bags. How about a fountain dedicated to Rudolph Valentino commissioned after his death by a group of loving fans? Learn about the "5-Globe Lewellyn," the "Olympic Special," and other historic streetlights still gracing the city's boulevards. These three compact books—Streetlights, Stairways and Fountains—designed as personal photo albums, convey the sense of discovery the author felt while pursuing her research. Experience your own sense of discovery as an armchair traveler touring Los Angeles' best urban details.

Streetlights

Published in the United States of America 2000

Design by Donna Milton
Imaging and production by Navigator Press, Pasadena, California
Printed in Hong Kong

Library of Congress Catalog Card Number: 00-131708
ISBN 1-890449-10-5

$14.95

ISBN 1-890449-10-5

9 781890 449100

Streetlights

Virginia Comer

BALCONY PRESS, LOS ANGELES

Lighting Los Angeles

Whether you are standing on a hillside or heading north on the 405 Freeway looking down into the San Fernando Valley, the evening view is dominated by lights, a blaze of electric lights, lending nighttime beauty to the City. Because the long and short-armed davit standards with the cobra head lamps are so common, it is easy to assume that all streets are lit by these stark, unimaginative light fixtures. Take another look. Daylight reveals a diversity of standards and lanterns. Occasionally, there is a mix of the historic with the contemporary; often there are enclaves of homes with the original street lamps.

In pueblo days of Los Angeles homeowners who lived on well-traveled streets were required to hang a lighted lantern in front of their doors at dark. Pedestrians were obliged to carry their own lanterns to guide them in areas less well lit. In 1857 a new process for street lighting, called Aubin gas, was put before the Council but it took nearly a decade (May 5, 1866) to make the decision to grant a franchise for the creation of a gas works. A lamplighter would ride through the streets at dusk lighting the street lamps.

Late in 1882, after aggressive competition from the gas company, Los Angeles mayor, James R. Toberman, pushed a button to activate the current for a new electric lighting system making L.A., with a population of 12,000, the first city to be lighted entirely by electricity. Lighting was by means of carbon arc source lamps on masts 150 feet high. The City boasted that the high-masted lights were visible by mariners far out to sea. However, not everyone was pleased; there were arguments against the new lights. Led by the rival gas company, it was said that the new lighting would be hard on the eyes, produce optical illusions and color blindness; keep the chickens up all night; attract bugs and lightning and change the complexion of ladies in general.

In Downtown Los Angeles those high-masted lights, which lit the city from 1882–1885 were said to give full-moon illumination. In the spring of 1905 an estimated crowd of 80,000 flocked to Broadway to watch a parade celebrating the City's first incandescent ornamental system, installed by the Broadway Boulevard Improvement Association.

Along with changes of style in street lighting, significant progress continued to improve the incandescent lamp; 1915, tungsten filament in inert gases; 1937, sodium vapor; 1938, mercury vapor; 1950, fluorescent lamps; 1968, high-pressure sodium; 1968, metal halide. In had begun to replace some of the existing incandescent lighting. Though the general public has been aware for some time of the two different types of electric lighting, what may be less familiar is the difference in definition. An incandescent lamp has a filament in a vacuum heated by an electric current to produce the light. Light from a fluorescent lamp is produced by exciting certain chemicals with ultraviolet energy.

Lamps were originally designed in vertical lamp housings, a variation of the original lighting of a torch. These glass lamps have a wide variance in style and size, from the charming and modest "Windsor Square" lamp to the handsome and imposing "Ventura Special," a striking design that failed to meet the nocturnal requirements. In the more contemporary luminaire, the lamp head is referred to as a cobra and the reference is obvious. Increase in traffic and population has often led to less attractive lighting for the sake of safety. Light standards now stretch ungainly arms over streets to maximize areas of illumination. In sections of the city with high rates of vandalism, light fixtures complete with bulletproof shields are installed. Keeping street lights in operating condition helps to prevent not only the look of neglect in a neighborhood but also crime and accidents.

At the City's Bureau of Street Lighting Office of Field Operations, located at the corner of Santa Monica and Virgil, there is an impressive array of old street lanterns in bronze, red brass and cast iron with a variety of glass casings; one comes in a fetching rose color. For more than six years, examples of some of the city's historical and ornamental streetlights have been on temporary display in the parking lot of a shopping center at the intersection of Santa Monica and Vermont. Artist Sheila Klein, with the cooperation of the Bureau of Street Lighting, created a sampling of the city's streetlights. Twenty-five electroliers stand in a row, offering a glimpse of light poles in varying styles and heights. More than half the light fixtures still have their identifying mark-

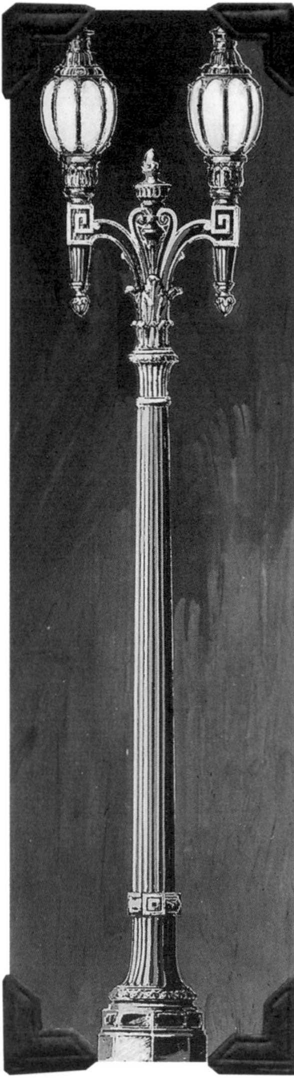

ers intact. A comprehensive look at street lighting is found in Eddy S. Feldman's *The Art of Street Lighting in Los Angeles* (Dawson Books, Los Angeles, 1972).

From the Five-Globe Llewellyn of the past to the cobra head of today, pedestrians have only to look up at the streetlights on the boulevards, avenues and streets of Los Angeles and recognize their place in the history of Los Angeles.

The Five-Globe Llewellyn

One of the distinctive streetlights of the early 1900s was the Five-Globe Llewellyn, which formed an attractive line of lights along Fifth Street in LA's downtown. This memorable photo was taken in the early 1900s when the Gothic building with the handsome wrought-iron canopy was known as the Temple Auditorium. In 1920 it became the Philharmonic Auditorium just across the street from the park we now call Pershing Square. The auditorium, with a seating capacity of 2,600, remained active until 1964 when the Music Center was built on Bunker Hill. Today a parking lot covers the space of the long demolished auditorium, and the Five-Globe Llewellyns are gone.

...ring st. looking South from Franklin st. at Night, Los Angeles, Cal.

The Five-Globe Llewellyn

In 1926 cars and trucks cross the Broadway Bridge, enhanced with tall arches and the Five-Globe Llewellyns.

Looming large in another area of Downtown Los Angeles this Five-Globe Llewellyn seems to dominate the street corner in 1940.

Standard Marbelite Pole

Marbelite, a stone-like concrete material, has been used for nearly 50 years in the creation of light standards. This slender pole, often a fluted column, has an aggregate surface which can be light or dark or a mixture inbetween. Marbelite light poles support a variety of lamps, one of the most common being an upright opaque globe with an acorn tip. This model is frequently seen on streets in historic residential areas such as Hancock Park and is the electrolier of choice at Pepperdine University in Malibu.

United Metal 1620

In this street scene of the 1920s, a vintage automobile parked by the United Metal 1620 light standard gives a time line to the elegantly simple light pole. A spare tire on the back of the auto in this photograph advertises motorcar sales and service. Both the vehicle and the passing streetcar in the background identify the era as the 1920s; the electric lamp is identified only as United Metal 1620, with a General Electric Form No. 12 lantern.

On another streetscape with vintage automobiles, a handsome street light is an example of the mix of lights and light standards. While the light standards in the photos are identical, the difference is in the number assigned to the lamps. This particular lamp is a General Electric Form No. 18.

United Metal No. 1620

An early 1940s photo taken at the corner of Second Street on Bunker Hill, before its major restructuring in the late 1950s to the 1960s displays a vintage streetlight with the unassuming designation of United Metal No. 1620 with the handsome G.E. Lamp No. 18. Like Victorian houses of the former residential community, this tall lamp with the impressive iron ornamentation is no longer found on the Hill.

A look at West Hollywood (Robertson and Rangely) in 1943, complete with contemporary billboard advertising Langendorf bread, shows streetlight UM No. 1620 standard with GE No. 12 globe.

The Broadway Rose

Downtown's Broadway, like its namesake in New York, has been an historical timepiece, marking the decades with changes in its commerce, its pedestrian traffic and its streetlights. In the spring of 1905 a parade celebrated the lighting of Broadway, between First and Tenth streets, with 134 iron lampposts which held a large globe at the top and six smaller ones in a circle below the central globe. To shield the powerful electric bulbs inside, all globes were opaque. In January of 1920 Broadway's 1905 lighting installation was replaced. The Los Angeles Times referred to Broadway as "The Radiant Way" and "the most brilliantly lighted street in the world." More than just brilliant lighting, the $100,000 installation featured lampposts with elaborate ornamental roses and Spanish renaissance designs. The lampposts known as the "Broadway Rose" have been refurbished recently by the City's Bureau of Street Lighting and can be seen on Broadway from Temple to Olympic streets. Contemporary lanterns, smoky glass spheres, on the "Broadway Rose" standard were replaced with General Electric No. 810 globes in a twin tear-drop design of the 1900s, used in the period between 1930s-1940s.

Twin Pendant Lamps

A long line of those twin pendant lamps on a bustling Broadway in 1956 reveals familiar shops of the past: Bullock's, Orbach's and Woolworth's. This popular light standard of the early 1900s, United Metal No. 1193, supported a number of different lamps.

United Metal No. 1906

Shown here the UM No. 1906 with the equally popular General Electric Form No. 18 towers over the fledgling palm bordering a street where autos of the 1920s travel.

The 1906 can often be seen supporting other styles of decorative globes.

Globe No. 124

Globe No. 124 in this photo of a tree-lined street with the vintage autos rests on a United Metal form No. 2500 offering yet another variation of combining different standards and lamps.

Washington and Hill Streets

In the 1930s this United Metal No. 1193 with another of the variety of lamps is in the foreground of the area of Washington and Hill Streets. The large building in the background is the Washington Furniture Company and the domed building in the left corner is the California Lutheran Hospital on Hope Street.

Angels Flight

At the corner of Third and Hill streets, the Five-Globe Llewellyn stands at the site of Bunker Hill's Angels Flight Incline Railway. This photo dates to the 1920s when the little funicular carried pedestrians up and down the hill's steep ascent from the Victorian enclave of residences to the commerce of Hill Street.

Both the Five-Globe Llewellyn and the equally handsome Victorian electrolier UM No. 1906 share lighting duties at the busy intersection of Third and Hill streets, site of popular Angels Flight funicular. This photo, taken by Bunker Hill resident T.S. Hall in 1940, shows that changes at the intersection had not included a change of street lighting.

A photo of the same site today would bear no resemblance to these earlier scenes.

Lights   Ted Helf
A.F. 1940   Photo
a Combination
of street lights in the busy
intersection of 3rd & Hill
streets

United Metal No. 1193

Since their inception, distinctive street lights defined an era. While some of the electroliers were specifically designed and named, others were ordered from a catalogue, indicated only by a number. Even with a specific name or number similar Victorian standards can still be confused. The United Metal No. 1193 bears a striking resemblance to United Metal No. 1906 which stands a lofty 24'3" compared to the 17'6" height of the United Metal No. 1193. Other differences can be found in the design in the center of the supporting arms of the standard and in its base.

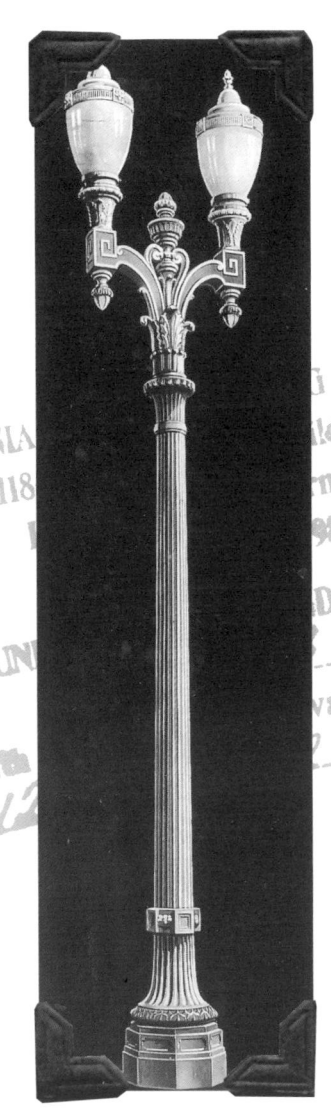

The Plaza of El Pueblo De Los Angeles

In the Plaza of El Pueblo de Los Angeles Historic Park, approximating the birthplace of the city, there is an example of the 1900s Five-Globe Llewellyn light fixture. In the late 1990s more than half a dozen light fixtures in the El Pueblo Historic Park were painted bright turquoise on the poles and a mustard color on the ornate supporting arms ostensibly to make them more festive in color. These fanciful lights flanked the area of the Plaza's old bandstand with its graceful Victorian wrought-iron siding.

Union Station

Architect Donald B. Parkinson designed the landmark Los Angeles Union Station, a cluster of low stucco, tile-roofed buildings, combining Spanish Mission and Moderne styles, topped by a 135-foot clock tower. Located on 52 acres of land, Union station is one of the last of the great American railroad stations. Opened with show-business fanfare in May 1939, the station had to compete with the advent of improved highway conditions and the growing popularity of air transportation. Once a favorite arrival and departure point for legends of Hollywood, Union Station began a decline in the number of passengers. Today Metro-rail, Metrolink and Amtrak use the refurbished station. Visible from Los Angeles and Alameda streets are the handsome twin pendant ornamental electroliers in front of the still grand Union Station.

Union Station early 1900's pole &
lamps
Courtesy: City of L.A. Bureau of
Street Lighting

The Victoria Park Fixture

Districts which prefer to have a special street light fixture pay an assessment for their choice. A 1920s photograph highlights one of the most unusual street fixtures with a light standard of elaborately scrolled iron holding four pendant globes with a larger light globe in the center. Clearly a special, the Victoria Park fixture, as the street sign indicates, is located at the corner of Victoria Park Road and Victoria Park Place.

The Wilshire Special

The Wilshire Special can be seen in a contemporary photo of MacArthur Park bisected by Wilshire Boulevard. In the early 1950s Westlake Park, in the western district of Downtown Los Angeles, was renamed MacArthur Park for the renowned general in a pique of patriotic fervor. When the park was refurbished, the historic streetlights with ornate electroliers at seven feet tall were kept intact. In 1928 the special lights were installed on Wilshire from Park View to Fairfax, the bronze lanterns of wired rock crystal were seven feet high and weighed four hundred pounds; the poles, cast iron covered with zinc and sprayed with bronze metal, weighed 1200 pounds. When these poles are replaced, cast aluminum is substituted for the cast iron.

The Westwood Special

These attractive light fixtures date from the early days of the University they honor. While regulation lighting—long concrete poles with twin cobra heads—has replaced many of the Westwood Specials, twenty new fixtures have been restored from Broxton to Le Conte at Westwood Boulevard. The electrolier is a very large, multi-paned lantern which rests on top of a blue pole, the base of which has rows of gold-colored tiles edged with blue. A contemporary photo offers a look at the attractive fixture with the colorful tiles while a second photo shows the same street lighting in an earlier time.

The Hollywood Special

As tourists saunter along Hollywood Boulevard, they tend to look down to read the names of the stars on the Hollywood Walk of Fame. A glance upward would reveal more stars on the streetlights. Towering above the Hollywood Walk of Fame is the high-masted Hollywood Special which features a long lamp in the form of a seven-foot shoe-box-style tri-light with five gold stars on the side. This star-spangled box lights up the night on Hollywood Boulevard east to Gower and west to Sycamore. With its gilded stars, this Hollywood Special directly in front of Graumann's Chinese Theatre, is in its element on the famed boulevard.

The Los Angeles Times Special

Another special lighting fixture in another well-known part of town, the Los Angeles Times Special, can be found in the historic block from Second to First streets on the corner of First and Main and First and Spring near the Los Angeles Times building. The unique streetlights have smoky bronze colored lamps on the same ornate light standard as the city's historic electrolier across the street. This present-day photo offers a look at the past with a light fixture of the 1900s, whose official name is UM 1906. LA's distinctive City Hall is the background in this photo looking north on Spring Street from the corner of Second.

L A Times Special Downtown LA
Second & Spring – 2 elements of
street lights, historical & contemporary
Courtesy LA City Bureau of Street Lights

Melrose Hill

Melrose Hill, on Oxford just off of Marathon, is a neighborhood of historic significance relating to the California bungalow at a time when California was known as the "bungalow capital of the world." A number of modest homes, built between 1911 and 1926, offers a time line of the bungalow phenomenon from the shingled cottages of the teens to the Spanish style of the '20s. Melrose Hill has its own distinctive light fixture, a medium pole supporting an attractive wrought iron-encased light globe.

Downtown

This contemporary skyview of a street light in downtown Los Angeles demonstrates the existence of vintage street lighting with the 1620A pole and General Electric No. 18 lamp. Another vintage fixture, the 1193 pole with a General Electric lamp No. 9, is in stark contrast to its background, which shows the Biltmore's modern addition at the southeast corner of Fifth Street and Grand Avenue. Offering another version, this short-armed davit with cobra head strikes a powerful pose against the glittery facade of a prominent high-rise on Bunker Hill.

Downtown

A contemporary photo of the restructured Bunker Hill shows Grand Avenue illuminated by a chorus line of davit poles, with short arms and cobra-head lights, arching in a slim canopy over the street.

West Hollywood

Along Santa Monica Boulevard in West Hollywood the street is lined with distinctive light poles painted a marine blue. The lamps on these brightly colored poles are spheres about the size of a basketball encaged in ornamental iron the same blue color as the poles. Under the supervision West Hollywood, not the Los Angeles Bureau of Street Lighting, the street poles match the blue of the benches at bus stops.

Mt. Hollywood Hiking Trail

A more staid presentation of light fixtures is this marbelite lamppost with a ubiquitous opaque lamp with an acorn tip. As the sign says, the fixture stands at the entrance to the Mt. Hollywood Hiking Trail in Griffith Park.

The Olympic Special

A view from this bridge brings the Olympic Special into focus against the background of a Downtown cityscape. The distinctive lamp pole, located at Olympic Boulevard and the City Hall Mall, was designed for the 1932 Olympics when Tenth Street was renamed Olympic Boulevard in honor of the world event.

The Sixth Street Bridge

A look at the Sixth Street Bridge in 1934 shows a different style of streetlights. A large lantern is perched on an Art Deco concrete pole featuring decorative relief. These fixtures were unique to this bridge.

6th H. Bridge 1934

The Shakespeare Bridge

A pendant lamp hangs from a small crook-shaped arm attached to the small tower on what is known as the Shakespeare Bridge. Built in the 1920s and declared Historical Cultural Monument No.126 in 1974, there is no clear historical evidence relating to the familiar naming of the Franklin Bridge as the Shakespeare Bridge. It is believed that its Gothic style with four small church-like spires at each end is reminiscent of the England of Shakespeare's period. What is clear historically is that there were originally eight vintage lamps on the Franklin Avenue Bridge. The Bureau of Engineering, which recently completed retrofitting of the bridge, intends to replace the missing lamps on the bridge.

Shakespeare (Franklin) Bridge
vintage lampposts

The Author

Historian Virginia Comer is widely published on the subject of Los Angeles history. Her books include *Angels Flight: A History of Bunker Hill's Incline Railway*, *El Alisal*, and *In Victorian Los Angeles—The Witmers of Crown Hill*, which won the Southern California Local History Award.

Acknowledgments

Grateful acknowledgment is given to the Historical Society of Southern California for the HSSC/Haynes Research Stipend; to the Bureau of Street Lighting, especially Engineering Technician Dwight Garcia, Assistant Director Philip Reed, Arthur Newborn, Electrical Supervisor; Tom La Bonge for taking time to photograph; Sally Beck and Virginia Neeley of the Huntington Library for assistance in identification of historic photographs and to Marc Wanamaker of Bison Archives for generosity with his time, talent and use of photos.

Picture Credits